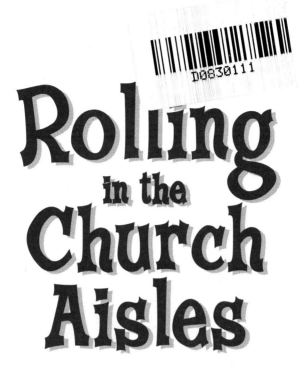

Rolling in the Church Aisles

Publications International, Ltd.

Illustrator: Amanda Haley

Contributing Writers: Rebecca Christian, Kelly Cison, Lawrence Greenberg, Ellen Pill, Angela Sanchez, Terri Schlichenmeyer, Paul Seaburn, Kim Sloane, Carol Stigger, Niki Taylor, Lynda Twardowsky, Kathy Yonce

Louis Weber, CEO
Publications International, Ltd.
7373 North Cicero Avenue
Lincolnwood, Illinois 60712

ISBN-13: 978-1-4127-1770-0
ISBN-10: 1-4127-1770-1

Manufactured in USA.

8 7 6 5 4 3 2 1

When there's something funny going on in church, it's a good thing!

Laughter and joy can be found anywhere you worship...in church bulletins, sermons, Sunday school lessons, even in the parking lot or the Fellowship Hall after services. A spiritual smile spreads happy faith far beyond the doors of church. So laugh your way through the day with some holy humor.

A minister is driving home one night when a police officer stops him for speeding. The officer smells alcohol on his breath, sees an empty wine bottle on the floor, and asks, "Sir, have you been drinking?" The minister replies, "Just water." The officer asks, "Then why do I smell wine?" The minister looks at the bottle and exclaims, "Good Lord! He's done it again!"

✳ ✳ ✳

Don't Worry About the Economy: Church Is Still Prophet-able.

God looks out at the Pearly Gates and says, "Welcome to heaven. I want the women to go with St. Peter and the men to form two lines here. All men who think they were in charge of their relationship on earth stand here, and the men who believe their wife was in charge, stand here."

There's much movement, but eventually the women are gone and there are two lines left. The line of the men who were not in charge is miles long. In the other line stands just one man.

God turns to this man and says, "You're the only one in this line. How did you manage this?"

The man shrugs and says, "I don't know; my wife told me to stand here."

Dear Pastor,
I know God loves everybody, but he never met my sister.

Arnold, age 7

CHURCH

Mr. Bradford was elected and has accepted the office of head deacon. We could not get a better man.

CHURCH HAPPENINGS

There will be a rummage sale next Saturday. Ladies, please leave your clothes in the basement.

❋ ❋ ❋

A man survives a shipwreck and finds his way to a small deserted island. He is able to survive there for more than three years until he is finally discovered. His rescuers are amazed at not only how well he survived but also at the small structures he was able to construct.

"What are those three little buildings?" they asked him.

"The one in the middle is my house," he replied, "and the one to the west is my church. The one on the east is the church I used to go to."

Sammy asked his mother if he could fill his little plastic pool with water, and since it was such a nice day, she agreed. Looking out the kitchen window, Sammy's mother was amused to see him lift the family's dog into the pool, then watched as he quickly dunked the dog's head and let it out a moment later. Next, he went and got the family's pet rabbit out of its hutch and did the same thing. Sammy's mother was getting very curious, although it was obvious he wasn't harming his pets. She went back to her chores until Sammy came running into the house.

"Mommy, can you please help me? The cat doesn't want to be baptized."

A little girl became restless as the preacher's sermon dragged on and on. Finally, she leaned over to her mother and whispered, "Mommy, if we give him money now, will he let us go?"

❋ ❋ ❋

CHURCH NOTES

Visitors of all abominations are invited to take communion and to join us in the Fellowship Hall for coffee and donuts.

An evangelist and a pastor were out in the woods hunting deer together, when suddenly a grizzly bear appeared and began to chase them. They raced back to their little hut, and the evangelist wrenched the door open. The pastor rushed inside and, unfortunately for him, the bear followed. Immediately the evangelist slammed the door shut from the outside.

"What are you doing?" the pastor screamed from inside the hut.

"I just bring them in, and then they're all yours!" called the evangelist.

Dear God,

*I think you'd be proud of me!
So far today I've done all right.
I haven't gossiped, lusted, lost my
temper, or been greedy, grumpy,
nasty, selfish, or overindulgent.
I'm very thankful for that.*

*In a few minutes, though, I'm going
to get out of bed. From then on I'm
probably going to need a lot of help.*

Amen.

✳ ✳ ✳

"Every evening I turn my
worries over to God. He's going
to be up all night anyway."

MARY C. CROWLEY

An old man had passed on. A wonderful funeral was in progress, and the country preacher talked at length of the good traits of the deceased, what an honest man he was, and what a loving husband and kind father he was. Finally, the widow leaned over and whispered to one of her children, "Go up there and take a look in the coffin and see if that's your pa."

✳ ✳ ✳

"Your Holiness," a cardinal gasped as he ran into the pope's office, "Jesus just rode into the Vatican on a donkey. What do we do?"

The pope looked up from his work and replied, "Look busy."

THIS WEEK'S SERMON

Reverend Kendra liked to add a little spice to her sermon about Jesus raising Lazarus from the dead. As she preached, she walked through the congregation waking up all of the snoozers.

✳ ✳ ✳

When Jacob's parents gave him his weekly allowance, he gave it to his little brother.

"Why did you do that?" his mom asked.

"I already have $75, and my Sunday school teacher said it is easier for a camel to go through the eye of the needle than for a rich man to go to heaven," Jacob said. "I don't want to be rich. I want to go to heaven."

CHURCH HAPPENINGS

The blessing of the pets will be followed by a hot dog lunch.

✳ ✳ ✳

Finding himself lost in the mountains on a cold Friday night, a man prays for the Lord's guidance and is led to a monastery. He is welcomed in, just in time for dinner. He is served a wonderful meal of fish and chips—the finest he has ever had, in fact. He asks if he may meet the cooks so he can thank them for the food.

When he tells them how much he enjoyed the meal, they thank him and introduce themselves.

"You're most welcome, friend. I am Brother Vincent, the fish friar, and this is Brother Paul, the chip monk."

A mortal said to God, "What is a million years like to you?"

God answered, "Like one second."

The mortal asked, "What is a million dollars like to you?

"Like one penny," God asked.

"Can I have a penny?" asked the mortal.

"Just a second," God replied.

✳ ✳ ✳

Try our Sundays.

They're better than

Ben & Jerry's.

A grouchy old man walks into the local church and proclaims to the administrative assistant, "Look here, you fool woman, I'm here to join this church."

The woman is shocked, sure she misheard. "Excuse me, sir?"

"Listen up, you fool woman, I am here to join this church."

The secretary stands up and declares she will not be spoken to that way. She goes into the pastor's office to explain the situation, and they both come out to the reception area together. The pastor addresses the man. "What seems to be the problem, sir? You can't just talk to my staff like that. Who do you think you are?"

"I didn't think there would be a problem," the man said belligerently. "I just won $200 million in the lottery, and this fool woman is trying to give me a hard time about joining this church. I'm just trying to

find a good place to get rid of some of this money."

"Well," said the pastor, "As soon as I escort this fool woman off of the property, you and I will sit down and get you all settled here at your new church."

※ ※ ※

CHURCH HAPPENINGS

The Seniors' group is sponsoring a picnic this Saturday. Each person is asked to bring a friend, a vegetable, or a dessert in a covered dish.

One day, three men were hiking in the wilderness when they came upon a large, raging river.

The first man prayed to God, saying, "Please God, give me the strength to cross this river."

Poof! God gave him big arms and strong legs, and he was able to swim across the river, although it took him a long time to make it, and he almost drowned a couple of times.

Seeing this, the second man prayed, "Please God, give me the strength and the tools to cross this river."

Poof! God gave him a rowboat, and he was able to fight the current and just manage to row across the river, after almost capsizing the boat a couple of times.

The third man had seen how this worked out for the other two, so he also prayed to God, "Please God, give me the strength, the tools, and the intelligence to cross this river."

Poof! God turned him into a woman. She looked at the map, hiked upstream a couple of hundred yards, then walked across the bridge.

* * *

THIS WEEK'S SERMON

Tonight's sermon topic is "What Is Hell?" Come early and listen to our choir practice.

There was a knock on the Pearly Gates, and St. Peter answered to find a man standing there. He glanced down at his clipboard to begin the intake process; however, when he looked back up, the man was gone. St. Peter shrugged and closed the gates. A moment later the same man knocked again. When St. Peter noticed him, he began to speak, but the man disappeared even as the saint was looking right at him. When the man appeared for the third time, Peter shouted, "Hey, what's the big idea? Are you trying to be funny?"

"No!" the man called back as he disappeared again. "They keep trying to revive me!"

❋ ❋ ❋

CHURCH HAPPENINGS

Attend a National PRAYER & FASTING Conference this Friday at 7:00 P.M. Sign-up fee includes meals.

One day Satan challenged God to a baseball game.

"You don't have a chance," answered God. "I have Mickey Mantle, Joe DiMaggio, Lou Gehrig, and all the greats."

"Well, that may be true," boasted Satan, "but I have all the umpires."

✳ ✳ ✳

A woman went to the post office to buy stamps for her Christmas cards. When it was finally her turn, the clerk asked her what denomination stamps she needed.

"Oh, for heaven's sake! Has it come to this? All right," the woman conceded. "Give me 25 Protestant and 25 Catholic."

An inexperienced preacher was to hold a graveside burial service at a pauper's cemetery for an indigent man with no family or friends. Not knowing where the cemetery was, the preacher made several wrong turns and got lost. When he eventually arrived, the hearse was nowhere in sight, the backhoe was next to the open hole, and the workers were sitting under a tree eating lunch.

The diligent young pastor went to the open grave and found the vault lid already in place. Feeling guilty because of his tardiness, he preached an impassioned and lengthy service, sending the deceased to the great beyond in style.

As he returned to his car, he overheard one of the workers say to the other, "I've been putting in septic tanks for 20 years, and I ain't never seen anything like that."

Dear God,
I thank you for my baby brother, but what I prayed for was a puppy.

Rachel, age 7

❋ ❋ ❋

After a night of swatting bugs on their camping trip, Keisha asked her mom, "How did two mosquitoes survive the entire trip on Noah's ark?"

On their way to the church service, a Sunday school teacher asked her pupils, "And why is it necessary to be quiet in church?" One bright little girl replied, "Because people are sleeping."

❋ ❋ ❋

"I know what Mary sang when Jesus brought home pictures from school," Tony told his parents. "How Great Thou Art."

Father Jim and Father Dale liked to play golf together because there was always a priest nearby to forgive them for swearing.

✳ ✳ ✳

CHURCH HAPPENINGS

Please join us at Saturday night's social and help our organizers, Adam and Eve, get things started.

✳ ✳ ✳

As Stuart tidied up the kitchen after dinner, he realized the broom had been left outside on the porch. "Cindy, go out back and get the broom, please." Cindy was scared and reminded her dad she was afraid of the dark. "Don't worry, Cindy, Jesus is out there to watch over you."

Cindy went over to the back door, opened it a crack, and whispered, "Jesus, could you please hand me the broom?"

CHURCH

In order to defray the cost of churchyard maintenance, it would be appreciated if those who are willing would clip the grass around their own graves.

✳ ✳ ✳

When Amber's mother took her to visit family graves on Memorial Day, Amber was keenly interested in inscriptions on tombstones, as well as the names and dates. Her mom explained that the dates indicate the day of birth and death. When they got to one pair of tombstones, a husband's and a wife's, Amber asked why there was no death date for the wife. Her mother explained that the woman hadn't died yet. Amber looked horrified and demanded, "Why did they bury her, then?"

A little girl was in church with her mother when she realized she was going to be sick. She tugged on her mom's arm and whispered, "Mommy, I need to leave right now! I'm going to be sick."

"Oh, dear, run down the hallway to the ladies restroom. You know where it is. When you're done, come back quietly."

The little girl scurried out and soon returned to the pew.

"Well, that was fast," her mom said. "Were you sick?"

"Yes, Mommy, but I didn't even have to go all the way down the hall. Right outside the chapel there is a box labeled, "For the sick.""

One Sunday afternoon a drunk stumbles across a baptismal service down by the river.

He proceeds to walk down into the water and stand next to the preacher.

The minister turns and notices the old drunk and offers, "Mister, are you ready to find Jesus?"

The drunk looks back and says, "Yesh, Preacher, I sure am."

The minister then dunks the fellow under the water and pulls him right back up. "Have you found Jesus?" the preacher asks.

"Nooo, I haven't," says the drunk.

The preacher then dunks him under a bit longer this time, brings

him up, and says, "Now, brother, have you found Jesus?"

"Noooo, I have not, Reverend."

The preacher sighs and holds the man under a little bit longer this time, brings him out of the water, and asks, "My God, man, have you found Jesus yet?"

The old drunk wipes his eyes and says to the preacher, "Are you sure this is where he fell in?"

✳ ✳ ✳

"**R**everend, I hope you didn't take it personally when my husband walked out during your sermon."

"Well, is everything all right?"

"Oh yes," answered the embarrassed wife. "Joe has been sleepwalking for years now."

Steven, a Protestant, moved into an all-Catholic community, where he received a good Christian welcome. But these good Catholics did not eat red meat on Fridays during Lent, so when their new neighbor began barbecuing a juicy steak on Friday night, they began to squirm.

They decided to talk to Steven about it. After much discussion, they convinced him to become Catholic. The next Sunday the priest sprinkled holy water on him and said, "You were born Protestant. You were raised Protestant. But now you are Catholic."

But the next Friday, as the neighbors sat down to eat their fish, they were once again disturbed by the smell of roast beef coming from the neighboring house. They went over to talk to the new Catholic to remind him he was not supposed to eat beef on Fridays.

When they got there, he was sprinkling ketchup on the beef and saying, "You were born a cow. You were raised a cow. But now you are a fish."

J anice woke up her son one Sunday morning and told him he needed to get ready to go to church. The son pulled the covers over his head and moaned, "Leave me alone. I don't want to go to church this morning."

"Nonsense," she replied. "Get up and get dressed."

"But everybody hates me, the sermons are boring, and none of my friends ever come," he whined.

His mother sighed and said, "Son, you have to go—you're the pastor!"

OUR CHURCH TODAY

For Easter services, we will ask Mrs. Brown to come forward and lay an egg on the altar.

✳ ✳ ✳

A mother gives her son two quarters when she signs him in at the Children's Ministry room at church. One is for the collection plate, and one is for a donut after the service. He is playing with the two quarters during the lesson, and one drops out of his hand and rolls out of reach under the large stage. "Oh, rats," thinks the little boy. "There goes God's quarter."

The late Reverend Billy Graham told of a time early in his ministry when he arrived in a small town to preach a sermon. Wanting to mail a letter, he asked a young boy where the post office was. When the boy told him, Dr. Graham thanked him and said, "Why don't you come to the Baptist Church on Third Street this evening? I'll be preaching about how to get to heaven."

The boy replied, "Thank you anyway, sir, but I don't think I'll be there. You don't even know your way to the post office."

VOLUNTEER OPPORTUNITIES

The director of the Christmas pageant is still looking for wise men. No experience necessary.

A man wants to become a monk. He goes to the local monastery and is brought to see the abbot. The abbot tells the man, "If you want to become a monk, first you must stay in a room alone for two years without speech. Then you will come out and tell me two words. This will show me whether you should be a monk."

The man stays alone and silent for two years, then comes before the abbot. The abbot nods at him and asks, "What do you wish to say?"

"Room cold," the man answers, hugging himself and shivering.

The abbot shakes his head. "I'm sorry, but you need two more years."

Again the man goes into the room alone, stays silent for two years, and again comes before the abbot. The abbot says, "What can you tell me?"

This time the man says, "Food bad."

The abbot again shakes his head and tells the man, "Two more years."

The third time, the man says, "Bed hard." Back he goes for two more years. When he comes out for the fourth time and the abbot asks him, "What two words, my son?" The man says, "I quit."

And the abbot says, "No wonder. It's been eight years and all you've done is complain."

＊ ＊ ＊

THIS WEEK'S SERMON

Pastor Smith had practiced the vows with the bride and groom twice the night before. Yet when the wedding came, the bride said: "God has prepared me for you and so I will ever strengthen, help, comfort, and discourage you."

An engineer dies and reports to the Pearly Gates. St. Peter checks his dossier and says, "Ah, I'm sorry, sir—you're in the wrong place." So, the engineer reports to the gates of hell and is let in. Pretty soon, the engineer gets dissatisfied with the level of comfort in hell and starts designing and building improvements. After a while,

hell has air-conditioning and flush toilets and escalators, and the engineer is a pretty popular guy. One day, Satan calls up God and gloats, "Hey, things are going great down here. We've got air-conditioning and flush toilets and escalators, and there's no telling what this engineer is going to come up with next."

God replies, "What? You've got an engineer down there? There's been a mistake—he should

never have gone down there. Send him up here."

"No way," Satan says. "I like having an engineer on the staff, and I'm keeping him."

"Send him up here immediately," God thunders, "or I'll sue you."

Satan laughs uproariously and answers, "Yeah, right. And just where are you going to get a lawyer?"

✳ ✳ ✳

The three-car crash was more than a fender bender, but thankfully no one was hurt. Maybe it was due to the sign on the church across the street: "God specializes in surprise endings."

An ad for St. Joseph's Episcopal Church shows a picture of two hands holding stone tablets, on which the Ten Commandments are inscribed. The headline reads, "For fast, fast, fast relief, take two tablets."

✳ ✳ ✳

The bingo players hated when Father Jim called the numbers because he'd throw in things like "B-Holy! I-missed-you-in-church! N-joy-my-sermons! G-sus loves you! O-come-o-come-Emmanuel!"

38

Church Chuckles

Q: Who lived in the Garden of Eden?
A: The Adamses.

Q: What is an unclean spirit?
A: A dirty devil.

Q: Who was the greatest comedian in the Bible?
A: Samson. He brought the house down.

Q: What do you get when you cross an atheist with a Jehovah's Witness?
A: Someone who knocks at your door for no apparent reason.

Q: What did the Zen Buddhist monk say to the hot dog vendor?
A: Make me one with everything.

Q: How many Buddhist monks does it take to change a lightbulb?
A: It cannot be determined from the question. First, the lightbulb must show that it strongly desires change.

A little-known Bible story tells why the first man stopped sharing every thought and feeling with his wife.

One day in the garden, Eve turned to Adam and asked, "Does this fig leaf make me look fat?" Adam, not knowing any better, gave her an honest answer. Eve got depressed and reached for the nearest available food—an apple—and the rest...well, the rest is history.

Charles Spurgeon was one of the greatest preachers of all times, often filling halls with 6,000 to 8,000 people crowded in to hear him share the Gospel. One night, after he had delivered a particularly stirring message, a rather stern looking elderly woman waited among the throngs to speak with the great preacher. "I don't care for the way you preach the Gospel, sir. You are far too overweight; it does not become a man of God. You smoke cigars, which is a terrible witness for the Kingdom of God. You often get so worked up while preaching you even spit while speaking. I tell you, sir, I just do not like the way you share the Gospel."

"I see," said Spurgeon. "And tell me, madam, how do you share the Gospel?"

"Well, I don't," she stammered.

Spurgeon gazed at her and replied, "Well, I must say, I like my way better."

41

The minister performed a beautiful wedding ceremony and had been asked to give a speech at the reception also. The father of the bride went over to the minister and asked, "Would you like to begin your speech now, or should we let everyone enjoy themselves a little while longer?"

* * *

Dear Pastor,
I think they call them pews because they smell funny.

Gabby, age 8

CHURCH NOTES

Please keep the Handlys in your prayers. On their recent trip to the Grand Canyon, Martha broke her ankle while helping George pass large stones on a donkey.

❋ ❋ ❋

A devout Christian and an atheist had been friends since they were boys, and they never missed an opportunity to poke fun at the other's beliefs. The atheist, visiting his friend's family cabin, noticed a beautiful chart depicting the various constellations and stars of the heavens. He inquired who had made it.

"What do you mean who made it?" the Christian said wryly, teasing his friend. "Nobody made it. It just happened."

One night the church gathered for a special prayer meeting. The evening was a complete blessing, the worship music was sweet, and everyone was glad to have come. The pastor asked one of the ushers to close the meeting with one last prayer. Dave's prayer was so rich, so tender and moving, that the congregation got revved up all over again, and the meeting went on for another two hours. On the way home the pastor said to his wife, "I have known Dave to be a godly man of prayer, a faithful man who studies the Word daily, and a man never to turn down an opportunity to serve the Lord, but today I learned something new about him."

"What's that, dear?"

"I learned never to ask him to say the closing prayer again."

The owner of a bed-and-breakfast wanted to name his three available rooms after the Gospels. Not knowing which names to pick, he finally decided upon Matthew, Mark, and Luke. *Now,* he thought to himself, *if I could only come up with a name for the bathroom.*

❋   ❋   ❋

CHURCH HAPPENINGS

Joel and Diane are getting married! Let's help stock their new home. Join us for a panty shower this Sunday.

❋   ❋   ❋

Asked what she had learned during the service, little Jane replied, "A Christian should have only one spouse. This is called monotony."

Timmy and Michael raced to the old swimming hole on Grandpa's farm that their dad had been telling them about. Sure enough, there was a big tire hanging from an old oak tree, and the brothers began to argue over who would swing into the cool water first. Grandpa saw this as a good teachable moment.

"You know, Jesus would have wanted the other person to go before him, to experience the joy first," he told them.

"That's right, Grandpa," Timmy nodded in agreement. "Our Sunday school teacher tells

us that Jesus was always doing things for others."

Grandpa smiled, pleased that Timmy understood him.

Then Timmy leaned over and said quietly, "Mikey, today I am going to let you be Jesus first."

※ ※ ※

OUR CHURCH TODAY

On Saturday night when the Erickson family went out to dinner, they explained to their curious little boy why gratuities are given and how they are calculated.  The next day at church when the offering plate came around, he whispered loudly to his father, "Dad, how much are you going to tip Pastor Paul?"

When little Eloise went to visitation for her great aunt who had just passed on, she was startled to look in the casket and see the departed holding a Bible in her hands. "I knew Auntie prayed a lot and went to church all the time," she commented to her mother, "but that's really something that she was holding the Bible when she died!"

＊　＊　＊

"My friend Dahna is Hindu," Mira told her mom. "Can you get her some Reincarnation powdered milk?"

VOLUNTEER OPPORTUNITIES

The church choir will begin practice for the Christmas Cantata next Wednesday at 7:00 P.M. We have a special need for men's voices, but all parts are welcome.

A minister and a senator arrived at the Pearly Gates at the same time, and being a humble fellow, the minister motioned for the senator to speak with St. Peter first.

"Senator, we've been expecting you. Welcome! Please, step into this limo. It will take you to the finest mansion we have."

Next, the minister approached. "Hello, Pastor," St. Peter welcomed him. "Here comes the shuttle bus to take you to your economy suite."

"Wait a moment." The minister was mystified. "I have served the Lord faithfully for many years. An economy suite is my reward?"

St. Peter smiled as he replied, "Well, we get ministers up here regularly, but this is the first senator we've ever had."

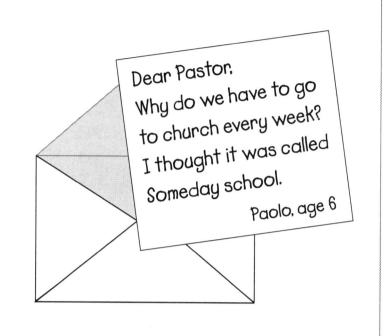

Dear Pastor,
Why do we have to go
to church every week?
I thought it was called
Someday school.

Paolo, age 6

✳ ✳ ✳

CHURCH HAPPENINGS

Our youth basketball team is back in action Wednesday at 8:00 P.M. in the recreation hall. Come out and watch us kill Christ the King.

Worried about the little country church's tough financial straits, its pastor asked the parishioners to dig deep into their pockets. "Dig deep," she said over and over as the collection plate was passed down the pews. "Dig deep!"

At the end of the service, a young boy tugged on the pastor's robe. "Did you get the money you needed for the church?"

The reverend shook her head sadly. "I'm afraid we didn't dig deep enough today, young man."

"I know just how you feel, Reverend Sonya. I've been in the backyard digging to China all summer, and I'm still not there either."

CHURCH NOTES

Couples preparing for marriage are asked to park behind the church hall for premarital classes.

✳ ✳ ✳

CHURCH HAPPENINGS

This afternoon there will be meetings in the south and north ends of the church. Children will be baptized at both ends.

OUR CHURCH TODAY

The teacher asked her Sunday school class, "Can anyone tell me why we call what we sit on in church a pew?"

Billy raised his hand. "Because sitting there next to your sister for a whole hour stinks?"

❊ ❊ ❊

A pastor known for his extremely lengthy sermons noticed a man get up and leave during the middle of his message. The man returned just before the conclusion of the service. Afterward, the pastor asked the man where he had gone.

"I went to get a haircut," was the reply.

"Why didn't you do that before the service?" the pastor demanded.

"I didn't need one then," the gentleman answered.

"I think I'll believe in Gosh instead of God. If you don't believe in Gosh, too, you'll be darned to heck."

AUTHOR UNKNOWN

A pastor said to a precocious six-year-old, "So your mother says your prayers for you each night? Very commendable. What does she say?" The little girl replied, "Thank God she's in bed!"

"**E**very day we're touched by God's miracles," said the preacher. "Who can give me an example of a miracle they've already witnessed this morning?"

Suzanne raised her hand.

"Have you witnessed a miracle today?"

"Yes," nodded Suzanne solemnly. "It took my big sister less than an hour to do her hair for church today."

❋ ❋ ❋

CHURCH HAPPENINGS

After Reverend Ray's talk entitled, "A Companion of Fools Shall Be Destroyed," join us in the meeting room, where a clown will entertain the children.

Nonexposure to the Son will cause burning.

＊　＊　＊

The deceased was a grouch and hated everybody. The minister skirted this point as kindly as he could when he opened the funeral service by saying, "Nearly beloved...."

There are angles all around us, hiding in every corner.

❋ ❋ ❋

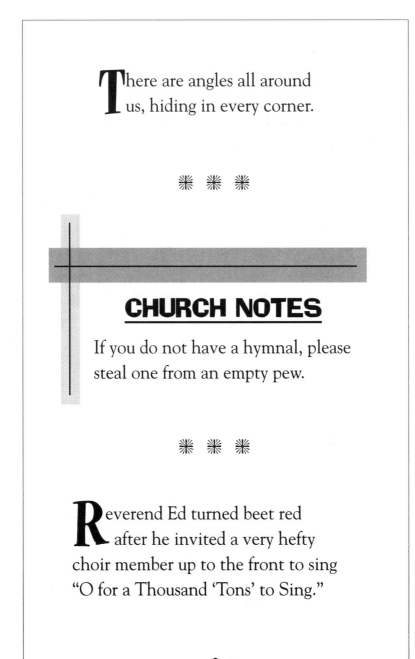

CHURCH NOTES

If you do not have a hymnal, please steal one from an empty pew.

❋ ❋ ❋

Reverend Ed turned beet red after he invited a very hefty choir member up to the front to sing "O for a Thousand 'Tons' to Sing."

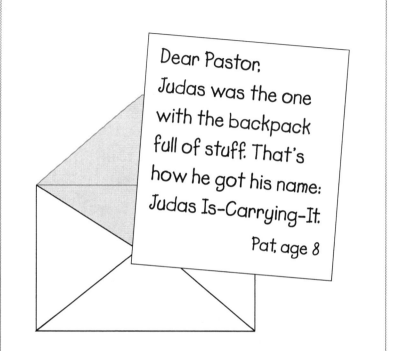

Dear Pastor,
Judas was the one with the backpack full of stuff. That's how he got his name: Judas Is-Carrying-It.

Pat, age 8

❉ ❉ ❉

Sixteen-year-old Mary stormed into the house and burst into tears: "If God is my copilot, how come I keep failing my driver's license test?"

After hearing about the Last Supper, little Alejandro said, "Jesus broke the bread? Wow, it must have been really stale!"

CHURCH

Missing: a purple lady's bicycle from the church parking lot.

CHURCH HAPPENINGS

BAKE SALE THIS WEEK (homemade breads our specialty)

SUNDAY SERMON: He Is Risen

※ ※ ※

Come in and pray today. Beat the Christmas rush!

Three clergymen had a standing tee time at the local golf course. One morning they arrived and found, much to their dismay, two men already there, wildly swinging golf clubs. The three clergy members went to the course manager and complained. The manager said, "Well, these two men came to me early this morning and said, 'We're blind and we'd like to see what it would be like to swing golf clubs.' So of course I couldn't refuse them."

The clergymen left.

The first said, "I'm ashamed. I was really angry. I will repent."

The second said, "I'm truly mortified. I was furious. I will do penance all day long."

And the third said, "Why couldn't they just play at night?"

OUR CHURCH TODAY

A Sunday school teacher said to her class, "We've been learning about how powerful the kings and queens were in biblical times. But there is a higher power. Who can tell me what it is?" Tommy blurted out, "I know! Aces."

※ ※ ※

CHURCH

Miss Charlene Mason sang "I Will Not Pass This Way Again" during the service, giving obvious pleasure to the congregation.

Dear Pastor,
Methuselah lived to be 969 years old because he was good at math and could count really high.

Harrison, age 8

✳ ✳ ✳

Samson could not understand why his parents were so against his new girlfriend. She did everything for him. Why, just this morning she even made an appointment for him at her favorite barber.

The church secretary thought she would surprise the pastor by redecorating his office while he was away at a retreat. She brought in a few plants, a new candle, and a nice pillow for the visitor's chair. The first change the pastor noticed when he returned was that his "IN" and "OUT" trays had been relabeled, "Prayer Requests" and "Prayers Answered."

✳ ✳ ✳

Sign on laundromat next door to a church:

> **Here's where cleanliness really is next to godliness!**

A preacher hit his stride in his sermon right around noon, and at that same time every Sunday, the train would go through town and blow its whistle. Several members of the congregation went to the train company and begged them to change the schedule. The darn whistle was waking everybody up!

※ ※ ※

"For two people in a marriage to live together day after day is unquestionably the one miracle the Vatican has overlooked."

BILL COSBY

OUR CHURCH TODAY

A mother was driving her three sons to church to be baptized. Jonathan said, "Mom, I'd really like to go first this morning, before Frank and Timmy."

"That's fine, dear," replied the mother, proud of her son's eagerness to begin a new life with the Lord.

"Thanks, Mom. I don't want my whole head under water that has all my brothers' rotten sins floating around."

Adam and Eve were very happy in the Garden, although Eve began to become suspicious of Adam when he suddenly began taking long walks in the evening. She tried to follow him a couple of times; however, she always lost him in the lush greenery. Every time he returned, Eve questioned him relentlessly. "Adam, where have you been? Have you been seeing another woman?"

"Eve, don't be ridiculous," came the same reply every night. "There are no other women."

This went on for weeks until one night Adam was awakened by Eve poking him sharply in the chest. "Eve, what in the world are you doing?"

"Counting your ribs," she answered.

✳ ✳ ✳

Jody looked up at a painting of God holding a lightning bolt and said, "Maybe the weather forecaster better start praying instead of predicting."

CHURCH NOTES

The Seniors Group will hear a
lecture about new evidence found
in the search for Noah's AARP.

✳ ✳ ✳

THIS
WEEK'S
SERMON

Being a baseball nut,
Reverend Oscar liked to
explain the Holy Trinity
as the world's greatest
unassisted triple play.

The minister had delivered a sermon on hell that would make the hair on the back of your neck stand up. Why, there wasn't a horror movie made that could compete with his description of the wailing and gnashing of teeth that awaited those who did not turn from their sins. One woman stopped to shake the minister's hand as she was leaving and remarked, "Reverend, I don't think I ever really knew what hell might be like until I heard you preach."

✳ ✳ ✳

If you can't sleep,

don't count sheep.

Talk to the Shepherd.

Kelly's parents were not churchgoers, so when she visited her aunt and uncle for the weekend, church was a new experience for her. When the congregation members were asked to bow their heads in prayer, Kelly nudged her aunt and whispered, "Wake up, Aunt Nancy! The teacher didn't say it was naptime yet."

"It's a good thing my Dad wasn't the one catching the fish the day Jesus fed the multitude," said Vicki. "The fish would have been a lot smaller than he told Jesus they were."

❋ ❋ ❋

Our pastor was winding down his sermon for the day. In the back of the church the fellowship committee stood to go to the church hall and prepare snacks for the congre-

gation. Seeing them get up, Pastor Miguel singled them out for praise. "Before they all slip out," he urged, "let's give these ladies a big hand in the rear."

A Jew, a Catholic, and an atheist are rowing on Lake Erie when their boat springs a huge leak. The Jew looks skyward and cries "Oh, Adonai, if you save me, I promise I'll sail to Israel and spend the rest of my days trying to reclaim the land you gave us."

The Catholic looks skyward and calls, "Oh, Jesus, if you save me, I promise I'll fly to the Vatican and spend the rest of my days singing your praises."

The atheist says, "Oh, guys, if you pass me that one life preserver, I promise I'll swim to Cleveland."

"And how will you spend the rest of your days?" the Jew and the Catholic ask.

"I'm not sure," answered the atheist. "But I can tell you one thing: I'll never go rowing with other atheists."

Stevie had just completed a drawing in Sunday school that he had titled "Moses." The teacher was impressed, and asked him which person in the picture was Moses. "Can't you tell?" said Steve. "He's the one in the mountain-climbing boots, carrying the fire extinguisher and bug spray."

Sign broken.

Message inside

this Sunday.

❋ ❋ ❋

VOLUNTEER OPPORTUNITIES

Come work for the Lord. The work is hard, the hours are long, and the pay is low. But the retirement benefits are out of this world.

Two church members were beginning to argue over how high to stack the chairs in Fellowship Hall. Finally one said, "Okay, look, here we are, arguing while we are serving the Lord. Let's do this. You work on that side of the room, doing it your way, and I will continue on this side of the room, doing it His way."

✳ ✳ ✳

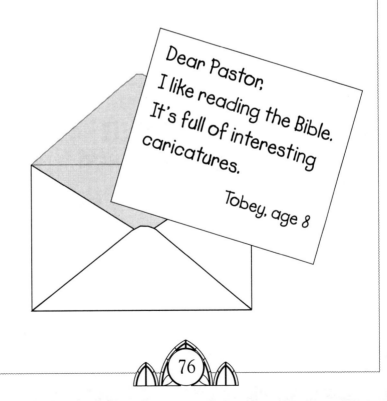

Dear Pastor,
I like reading the Bible. It's full of interesting caricatures.

Tobey, age 8

CHURCH HAPPENINGS

Because of our special silent devotional service, the pastor asks that you leave all crying babies at home.

✳ ✳ ✳

A man was brought from a retirement home to attend church one Sunday, and the pastor spent a moment speaking with him after the service. "It was wonderful to have you visit. I hope you are able to come again."

"Well, you talk too long, you talk too fast, and you never say anything new," the visitor said. "But I liked it anyhow."

Just then the man's aide rushed over and whispered to the pastor, "Reverend, pay no attention to Mr. Thomas. He isn't all there. He just repeats anything he hears someone else say and then ends it with, 'But I liked it anyhow.'"

One day Alex asked his mother for a new bike. His mother said, "At Christmas you send a letter to Santa to ask for what you want, don't you?"

"Yes," replied Alex, "but it isn't Christmas."

His mother said, "Yes, but you can send a letter to Jesus and ask him."

So Alex sat down with a pen and paper and started his letter:

Dear Jesus,
I've been a good boy, and I would like a new bike.
Your Friend,
Alex

Then he thought that wasn't quite right, and wrote a new letter:

Dear Jesus,
Sometimes I'm a good boy, and I would like a new bike.

That still wasn't right, so he decided to write another letter:

> Dear Jesus,
> I thought about being a good boy, and I would like a new bike.

Then he thought he didn't like that one either. He got depressed and decided to take a break and go walk around. He passed by a house with a small statue of Mary in the front yard. He picked up the statue and hurried home. He put the statue under his bed and started his new letter.

Dear Jesus,
If you want to see your mother again, send me a new bike!
Your Friend,
Alex

The retiring Sunday school teacher left a note for her replacement warning that the Johnson triplets always started crying during the story of Noah loading up the ark.

✳ ✳ ✳

OUR CHURCH TODAY

The congregation found out about the organist's other job when, out of habit, he brought out an ashtray, a drink coaster, and a jar marked "Tips."

✳ ✳ ✳

Many people who knew Boaz were very glad to see him get married. Apparently, he was Ruth-less when he was a bachelor.